OhSewEasy
pillows
29 Projects for Stylish Living

Jean & Valori Wells

C&T PUBLISHING

Text © 2006 Jean Wells and Valori Wells

Artwork © 2006 C&T Publishing, Inc.

Publisher: Amy Marson

Editorial Director: Gailen Runge

Acquisitions Editor: Jan Grigsby

Editor: Candie Frankel

Technical Editors: Elin Thomas and Wendy Mathson

Copyeditor/Proofreader: Wordfirm, Inc.

Design Director/Cover/Book Designer: Kristy K. Zacharias

Illustrator: Kirstie L. Pettersen

Production Assistant: Kerry Graham

Photography: Diane Pedersen and Luke Mulks unless otherwise noted

Published by C&T Publishing, Inc., P.O. Box 1456, Lafayette, CA, 94549

Front cover: Front to back: Stitched Panel, Pieced Border I, Horizontal Panels, Basic Square, Horizontal Panels, Log Cabin I, Stitched Panel

Back cover: Clockwise from top: Whipstitched Squares, Easy Patchwork, Wool Circles, Envelope

Library of Congress Cataloging-in-Publication Data

Wells, Jean.

   Oh sew easy pillows : 29 projects for stylish living / Jean and Valori Wells.

     p. cm.

   Includes index.

   ISBN 1-57120-341-9 (paper trade)

   1. Pillows. 2. Machine sewing. I. Wells, Valori. II. Title.

TT410.W45 2006

746.9'7--dc22   2005017588

Printed in China

10 9 8 7 6 5 4 3 2 1

acknowledgments

Writing a book is always a big undertaking. It takes a team to pull it all together. Laura Simmons helped us stitch the pillows. Photographer Luke Mulks flew to Sisters and worked with us to capture the essence of our vision. Candie Frankel helped us organize and edit our manuscript. Kristy Zacharias brought our words and photos together in a beautiful format designed to appeal to today's new generation of sewers. Thank you especially to C&T Publishing for believing in our soft furnishing series and making this book possible.

contents

introduction

Pillows are everyone's favorite decorative accessory. Just a few pillows can infuse a room with new design, style, and color.

Oh Sew Easy Pillows

Pillows soften a room and invite relaxation. What is more comfortable than chatting with a friend on a sofa or reading at a window seat with a plush pillow at your back?

Pillow styles run the gamut. They can be extravagantly ornate or quiet and unobtrusive. Bright or high-contrast colors draw the eye and create excitment. A pillow can showcase your needlework or become a special gift. Because pillows are easy and inexpensive to make, you can change them with the seasons or anytime you want to experiment with new home decor.

We have designed the pillows in this book to reflect a variety of styles. The first chapter, "Pillow Talk," discusses the basics. You'll learn how to choose fabrics and pillow forms, how to measure for a proper fit, and how to sew a basic pillow cover. The second chapter, "Decorative Details," describes simple techniques you can use to give the pillows you sew your own unique design stamp.

And then come our pillow recipes: 29 fabulous designs in all, many of them to sew in multiple sizes using our easy-to-follow cutting guides. Each recipe features a color picture of the completed pillow along with how-to illustrations and simple instructions. Don't miss the jam-packed pillow gallery at the end, for even more color and fabric combinations to fuel your creativity.

Have fun!

Jean & Valori

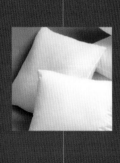

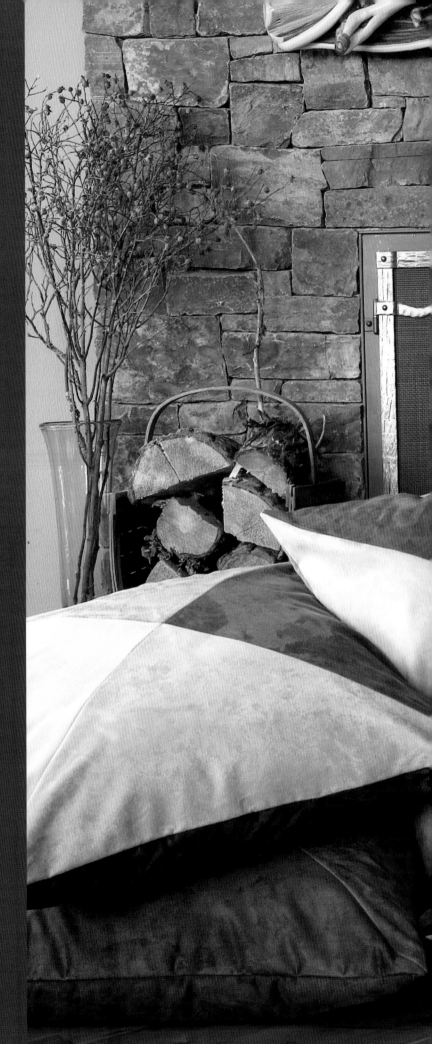

pillow talk

What is a pillow made of? What kinds of fabric can I use? What goes inside? In this chapter, we'll look at the essential parts of a pillow and learn how to put them together.

The Fabric Cover

Every pillow has an outer covering of fabric. You can use the same fabric on the front and the back, for a reversible pillow, or you can choose a decorative fabric for the front and a more utilitarian fabric for the back. You don't have to use just one fabric for the pillow front. Many exciting designs are created by sewing various fabrics together, patchwork style.

Which fabric you select for your pillows depends on the mood or ambiance you are trying to create. Because pillows are relatively small accents, you can use brighter, more intense colors for them than you would for larger furnishings such as slipcovers or draperies. A pillow is the perfect way to work a surprise accent color, a witty theme print, some intriguing patchwork, or a piece of needlework into the decor.

You should also consider the pillow's function. If the pillow will be used on a regular basis in an active area, such as a family room, choose a washable fabric with a tight, durable weave. Decorator fabrics, which include upholstery and drapery-weight textiles, are heavier and more durable than quilting cottons and can stand up to lots of wear. Some decorator fabrics are treated with Scotchgard to shed dirt, grime, and even liquid spills. Felted wool, either purchased or made at home by shrinking wool yardage, is another durable choice that offers depth of color and rich texture.

How to Felt Wool

Submerge 100% wool fabric briefly in boiling water. Lift it out with tongs and drain it in a colander. Lay the wool on an old, clean towel and roll it up to squeeze out the excess water. Put the wool in a washing machine and run the spin cycle to remove more of the water. Dry the wool in a dryer for about twenty minutes. This entire process pulls the wool fibers together and creates a dense, washable fabric that doesn't ravel.

For purely decorative pillows, less durable fabric can be chosen. Raw silk can bring elegant sophistication to a living room or bedroom. For casual rooms, there are broadcloth-weight cottons in a wide range of solids, prints, stripes, and plaids. The printed design and also the texture of a fabric can suggest popular styles, such as French country, vintage, lodge, retro, and tropical.

To add heft and surface texture, the pillow cover fabric can be padded on the underside with thin batting. Lightweight fusible batting is available by the yard. For small pillows or pincushions, scraps of batting can be used. The padding can be left as is or quilted with decorative stitching on the right side.

Working With Silk

To prevent silk fabric from raveling, iron lightweight woven fusible interfacing to the wrong side. Fusible interfacing can also be used to add body to delicate or drapey fabrics.

It all stacks up. When you cover assorted forms in coordinating fabrics, you avoid wasting yardage. The result is a handsome pillow set.

Pillow forms

The Pillow Form

You could simply stuff fiberfill, foam, or batting into a pillow cover and sew it closed, but the resulting pillow would be lumpy and difficult to wash. The professional approach is to use a pillow form. It can be removed and reinserted, allowing you to wash a pillow cover, or exchange one cover for another, with ease.

A pillow form looks like a plain pillow. The outer covering is usually white or off-white fabric. Stuffing materials include fiberfill, silk, and down and feathers. Spun polyester forms, with a surface resembling quilt batting, are also sold. For a fluffy pillow, choose a high-quality pillow form. Less expensive forms tend to flatten out with use because the fibers inside do not spring back after being compacted.

The pillow covers in this book are designed for square or rectangular forms. The square pillows range in size from 10″ to 30″. The rectangular pillows range from 12″ × 22″ to 14″ × 28″. Standard-size pillow forms are available at sewing, fabric, and home decor stores. For odd-sized pillows, you can make your own pillow form (see Making a Pillow Form on page 16).

Basic How-Tos
measuring up

Begin your pillow project by buying (or making) a pillow form in the desired shape and size. Then measure the form and calculate how much fabric is needed to cover it. Here's how you would proceed for a 16″ square pillow form:

1. Use a flexible tape measure to measure the pillow form from seam to seam, in both directions (width × length).

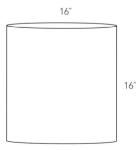

16″

16″

Pillow Form

2. For the pillow front, add ½″ to the pillow form width and length to allow for a ¼″ seam allowance on each edge. (For fabrics that are thick or prone to ravel, add 1″ to each measurement, for a ½″ seam allowance on each edge.)

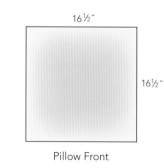

16½″

16½″

Pillow Front

3. For the pillow back, add ½″ to the pillow form length and 5″ to the pillow form width. Divide the width in half, for 2 pillow back pieces.

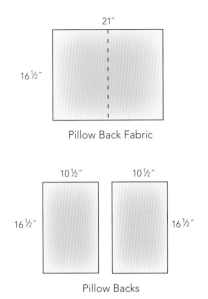

21″

16½″

Pillow Back Fabric

10½″   10½″

16½″   16½″

Pillow Backs

4. Draw a picture of the three pieces (one front and two backs) on graph paper to plan your cutting layout and figure the fabric yardage. In this example, the front and back pieces can be cut from ½ yard of 42″-wide fabric. Take your sketch with you when you shop for fabric. If the fabric you like is a different width, or if you decide to use one fabric for the pillow front and another fabric for the pillow back, you may have to refigure the yardage at the store.

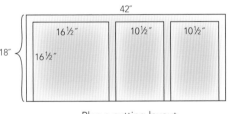

42″

16½″   10½″   10½″

18″   16½″

Plan a cutting layout

5. Use your dimensions and cutting layout to cut 1 pillow front and 2 pillow backs from the selected fabric. For accurate measuring and cutting, use a rotary cutter, grid ruler, and cutting mat.

Fabric Widths

Most broadcloth-weight cotton fabric is 42″ wide. Decorator fabrics range from 56″ to 60″ wide. Yardage requirements for the pillows in this book are based on a 42″ width. Less fabric may be required if you use decorator fabrics.

sewing

1. For a clean finish edge, fold one long edge of a pillow back ¼″ to the wrong side, fold again ¼″, and stitch the narrow hem. Press. Repeat for the other pillow back piece.

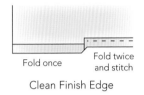

Fold once   Fold twice and stitch

Clean Finish Edge

2. Place the pillow front right side up on a flat surface. Place the pillow backs on top, right sides down, matching the raw edges to the pillow front. The narrow hemmed edges of the pillow backs will overlap by 2″, creating a concealed opening for inserting and removing the pillow form. Pin the raw edges.

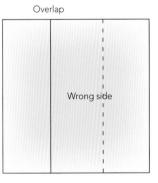

Overlap

Wrong side

Join the front and backs

3. Stitch ¼″ from the raw edges all around, pivoting at the corners.

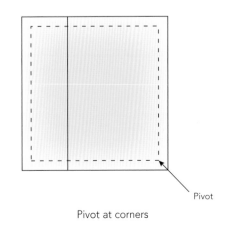

Pivot

Pivot at corners

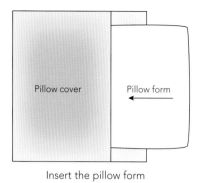

Insert the pillow form

How to Pivot

A pivot is a sewing maneuver that will help you create sharp corners on square and rectangular pillows. To gain control, slow down the sewing machine speed as you approach the corner. Stop sewing ¼" from the fabric edge with the needle in the down position. Lift the presser foot and rotate the fabric one-quarter turn. Lower the presser foot and continue sewing along the adjacent edge.

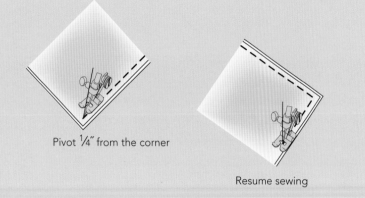

Pivot ¼" from the corner

Resume sewing

making a pillow form

1. Determine the size of the pillow form needed; in our example, we'll make a 9" × 12" pillow form. Add ½" to both measurements, for a ¼" seam allowance on all sides. Cut two pieces of tightly woven muslin to this size. You can also use ticking, duck, or any tightly woven cotton fabric for the pillow form.

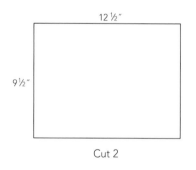

12 ½"

9½"

Cut 2

4. Trim the excess fabric from the corners. Press the seam allowance open as close to the corner as the tip of the iron will go.

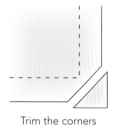

Trim the corners

5. Turn the pillow cover right side out. Press the front, back, and edges. Compress the pillow form and insert it through the opening in the back. Once the form is inside the pillow cover, adjust it so that it fills out the corners.

2. Layer the two pieces right sides together. Stitch ¼" from the edge all around, pivoting at the corners and leaving a 5" to 6" opening on one edge. Trim the corners.

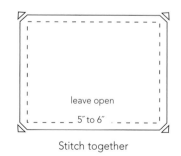

leave open

5" to 6"

Stitch together

3. Turn right side out. Fold in the loose raw edges at the opening and press well. Press the edges all around.

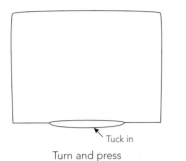

Tuck in

Turn and press

4. Fill the pillow with fiberfill or another loose stuffing material, a little bit at a time, to create loft in the pillow form. Fill the corners first and work in from there. Continue adding stuffing until you are satisfied with the amount of fullness. Pin the open edges together. Slipstitch closed.

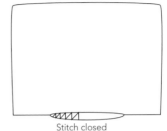

Stitch closed

Stuff until full and slipstitch closed

Pillows in floral prints make an outdoor twig bench comfortable and inviting.

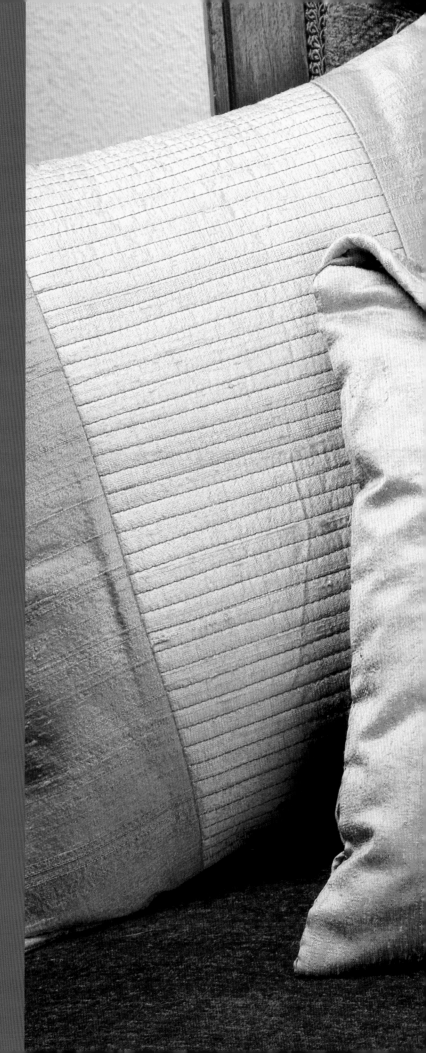

decorative details

Well-chosen details draw attention to the overall design of the pillow and, ultimately, the room.

FLANGE

A flange is a flat edge treatment that typically extends 1 to 2 inches beyond the edges of the pillow form. It appears to frame the pillow and is especially suited to crisp fabrics that can hold a crease. Because the flange is an extension of the actual pillow fabric, you achieve a decorative edge without buying any special braids or trims.

1. Decide on the finished width of the flange. Multiply the width by 2 and add ½″ to determine the extra allowance. The allowance for a 1″ flange, for example, is 2½″.

2. Add the allowance to the pillow form length and width to determine the dimensions of the pillow front. Cut the pillow front to these dimensions. Cut two pillow backs to correspond (see Measuring Up, steps 1–4, on pages 14–15).

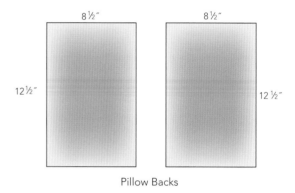

Pillow Backs

3. Sew the pillow front and backs together, turn right side out, and press well (see Sewing, steps 1–5, on pages 15–16).

4. Measure one flange width from each outside edge and lightly draw a line with a white chalk pencil. Stitch on the marked line through both layers of fabric all around, pivoting neatly at the corners.

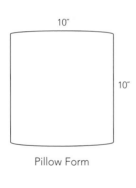

Pillow Form

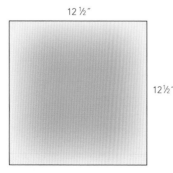

Pillow Front

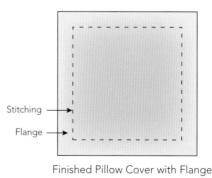

Finished Pillow Cover with Flange

5. Insert the pillow form through the back opening. The stitching line will contain the pillow form. The fabric beyond the stitching line will form the flange.

RUFFLE

A ruffle adds a frilly, feminine touch to a pillow. The fabric for a ruffle can match or contrast with the pillow front. Either way, the added volume and movement around the edges make the pillow appear bigger. A single ruffle uses one layer of fabric, and the raw edge is finished with a narrow hem. In a double ruffle, the fabric folds back on itself, so no hem is needed.

1. Decide on the finished width of the ruffle. For a single ruffle, add 1″ to the finished width. For a double ruffle, multiply the finished width by 2 and add ½″. The result is the width of the cut ruffle strip. The strip width for a 2″-wide double ruffle, for example, is 4½″.

2. Measure the four edges of the pillow form and add them together. Multiply the total by 2.5 to determine the ruffle length. The ruffle length for a 10″ × 10″ pillow, for example, is 100″.

3. Cut a strip to the appropriate width and length, as calculated in steps 1 and 2. Ruffle strips can be cut on the straight grain or on the bias. Piece several strips together as needed to obtain the required length (see Piping, steps 1–2, on page 23 for details on cutting and piecing bias strips).

4. Sew the ends of the strip together to make a loop. To hem a single ruffle, fold in one long edge ¼″, fold in again ¼″, and stitch. For a double ruffle, fold the looped strip in half, right side out and raw edges together, and press.

5. Machine baste 2 rows of stitches ⅛″ apart along the raw edge. Insert 4 pins along the stitching to divide the loop into 4 equal parts.

6. Draw up the bobbin threads fully to gather the ruffle. Place the ruffle on the pillow front, right sides together and raw edges matching. Align the pin markers to each corner. Pin all around, relaxing the gathers to fit. Machine baste in place. Join the pillow front and backs in a ¼″ seam, being careful not to catch the gathers in the seam.

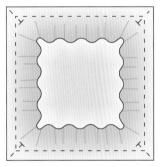

Attaching the ruffle

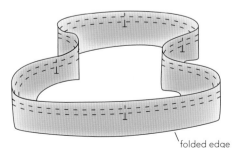

folded edge

Preparing the ruffle loop

CORDING

Cording is generally made of rayon or cotton. It comes in a variety of colors and its characteristic twist or braid adds texture and movement to the edge of a pillow. Cording is very easy to apply. The attached flat edge is sewn into the seam and disappears from view. Purchase enough cord to fit around the pillow plus 3 inches. Wrap a bit of masking tape around the ends of a length of cording to prevent raveling as you work.

1. Mark the middle of the bottom edge of the pillow front. Pin the flat edge of the cording to the pillow front, starting at the mark and leaving 1½″ of the cording free.

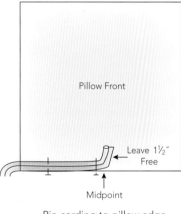

Pin cording to pillow edge

2. Pin all around, clipping into the flat edge for a smooth turn at the corners. Using a zipper foot, machine baste close to the cord all around. (For tips on using a zipper foot, consult your sewing machine manual.) When you reach the starting point, hold the free ends together and let them curve off the seam allowance as shown.

Clip cording at corners

3. Join the pillow fronts and backs using a zipper foot and stitching on the machine basting line. Clip the excess cording even with the seam allowance.

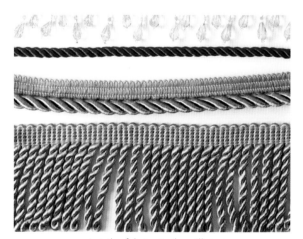

Let the fabrics in the pillow cover guide you to compatible trims.

PIPING

Piping is a fabric-covered cord that is sewn around the edge of a pillow the same way as cording. You can purchase ready-made piping, but for a unique accent, create your own using the fabric of your choice. You'll also need cotton piping cord, which is sold by the yard in a variety of sizes at fabric and home decorating shops. Purchase enough cord to fit around the pillow plus 3 inches. The fabric strips for this trim are cut on the bias to provide ease around curves and corners.

1. Measure around the cord with a flexible tape measure and add ½″, or enough for two seam allowances, to determine the strip width. Place the ruler on the fabric at a 45° angle. Cut several strips the required width.

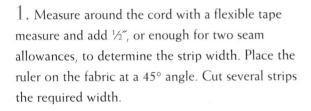

Cut bias strips

2. Sew the strips together end to end with diagonal seams. Press the seams open. Cut and add more strips if needed until the length is the same as the cord.

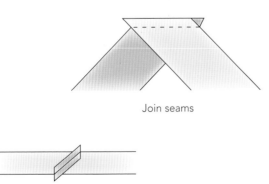

Join seams

Press open

3. Center the cord on the wrong side of the strip. Fold the strip over the cord, matching the raw edges. Using a zipper foot, machine baste close to the cord, starting and stopping 1½″ from each end. (For tips on using a zipper foot, consult your sewing machine manual.)

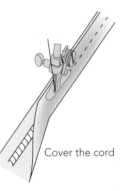

Cover the cord

4. Pin the piping to the pillow front, starting at the middle of one edge and matching raw edges. Clip into the piping seam allowance for a smooth turn at the corners. Start stitching 1½″ from one end of the cord. Stitch all around, stopping 2½″ from the starting point. Fold under the excess fabric strip, tuck it under the starting strip, and clip away any excess. Cut the cording so that the two ends butt together. Stitch the final 4″.

Join the ends

5. Join the pillow front and backs using a zipper foot and stitching on the machine basting line.

STITCHING

Decorative thread work, done either by hand or machine, adds quiet, under-stated texture to your pillow designs. Hand sewing gives pillows a crafty boutique look that invites touching. You don't have to be an expert needle artist to achieve great effects with blanket stitch or whipstitch and felted wool. For stitch illustrations, see pages 50 and 52.

Hand tying with perle cotton

Outline quilting by machine is especially rewarding. After you finish sewing the pillow front, place a piece of thin quilt batting underneath and work your stitching from the right side through both layers. Simply sew around the shapes that are printed on the fabric. For more maneuverability, drop the feed dogs on the machine and use a free-motion embroidery foot. You'll be able to move the fabric at will in any direction. Refer to your sewing machine manual for machine settings and practice the stitching on scrap fabric and batting before you tackle the pillow top.

Outline quilting designs repeated in a solid area

When you outline the same shape repeatedly, you will find that you begin memorizing the lines and your hand motion. This memory will enable you to duplicate the same shape freestyle in other areas of the pillow front. As you become more fluid with free-motion quilting, you'll be able to create your own designs.

Free-motion quilting of a leaf design

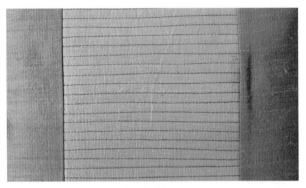

Diagonal grid on patchwork squares

For a more traditional look, try straight quilting. Use a standard presser foot. You can stitch in-the-ditch or in a grid pattern that complements the patchwork. Parallel stitching lines are easy if you use the edge of the presser foot as a guide for the next line of stitching.

Parallel lines

BUTTONS

Think of buttons as jewelry. You can sew them onto any pillow cover, singly or in multiples. Like fabrics, buttons can evoke particular styles. Plastic buttons are casual and easygoing. Vintage buttons make for interesting conversation and are fun to examine. You can use pillows to display the vintage treasures hiding in your button box. For the ultimate in luxury, use button-making kits, available at fabric stores, to create fabric-covered buttons that coordinate perfectly with your pillow-cover fabrics.

A faux tortoiseshell button coordinates beautifully with the warm colors in two companion pinecone prints.

pillow recipes

Find a style you like, buy some fabric, and start sewing! Our easy pillow recipes give you lots of size and color options to create your own custom designs. Yardage requirements are for 42″-wide fabric. Sew all seams with a ¼″ seam allowance. Press the seam allowance toward the darker fabric, except where noted.

basic square

This design uses the same fabric for the pillow front and back. Follow the Sewing instructions on page 15.

Materials and Cutting Guide

PILLOW FORM	FABRIC	FRONT (cut 1)	BACK (cut 2)
10″ × 10″	⅓ yard	10½″ × 10½″	10½″ × 7½″
12″ × 12″	⅜ yard	12½″ × 12½″	12½″ × 8½″
14″ × 14″	½ yard	14½″ × 14½″	14½″ × 9½″
16″ × 16″	½ yard	16½″ × 16½″	16½″ × 10½″
18″ × 18″	¾ yard	18½″ × 18½″	18½″ × 11½″
20″ × 20″	1¼ yards	20½″ × 20½″	20½″ × 12½″
24″ × 24″	1½ yards	24½″ × 24½″	24½″ × 14½″
30″ × 30″	1¾ yards	30½″ × 30½″	30½″ × 17½″

Materials

PILLOW FORM	FABRIC A	FABRIC B
12″ × 12″	¼ yard	¼ yard
16″ × 16″	½ yard	¼ yard
20″ × 20″	⅝ yard	¼ yard

Cutting Guide

PILLOW FORM	FABRIC A		FABRIC B
	PANEL A (cut 1)	BACK (cut 2)	PANEL B (cut 2)
12″ × 12″	6½″ × 12½″	12½″ × 8½″	3½″ × 12½″
16″ × 16″	8½″ × 16½″	16½″ × 10½″	4½″ × 16½″
20″ × 20″	10½″ × 20½″	20½″ × 12½″	5½″ × 20½″

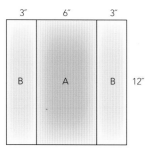

Pillow Front

PILLOW FRONT: Sew a B panel to each long edge of panel A. Press. Topstitch ¼″ from the seams with matching or contrasting thread.

ASSEMBLY: Follow the Sewing instructions on page 15.

vertical panels

Sew this two-tone design in silk (shown), cotton, or wool. If you choose silk, fuse lightweight woven interfacing to the wrong side to add strength and stability and to prevent the cut edges from raveling.

stitched panel

The middle panel in this design is textured with parallel rows of straight stitching. Place fleece under the center panel and quilt before adding the side panels. Use matching or contrasting thread.

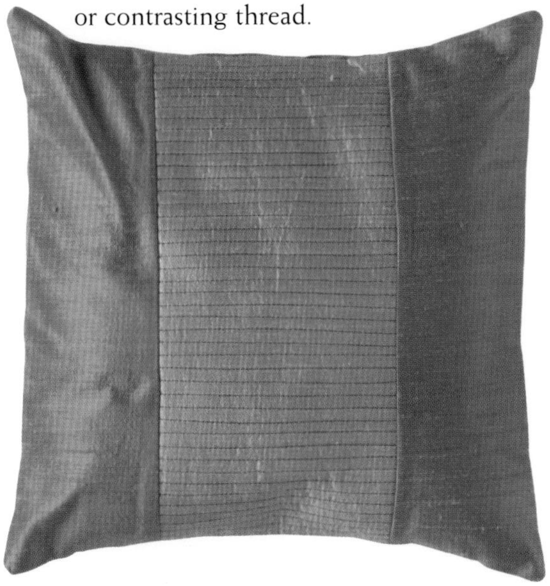

Materials

PILLOW FORM	FABRIC A	FABRIC B
12″ × 12″	¼ yard	¼ yard
16″ × 16″	¼ yard	⅓ yard
20″ × 20″	⅓ yard	⅝ yard

Cutting Guide

PILLOW FORM	FABRIC A		FABRIC B
	PANEL A (cut 1)	BACK (cut 2)	PANEL B (cut 2)
12″ × 12″	5½″ × 12½″	4″ × 12½″	12½″ × 8½″
16″ × 16″	7½″ × 16½″	5″ × 16½″	16½″ × 10¹⁄₁₂″
20″ × 20″	9½″ × 20½″	6″ × 20½″	20½″ × 12½″

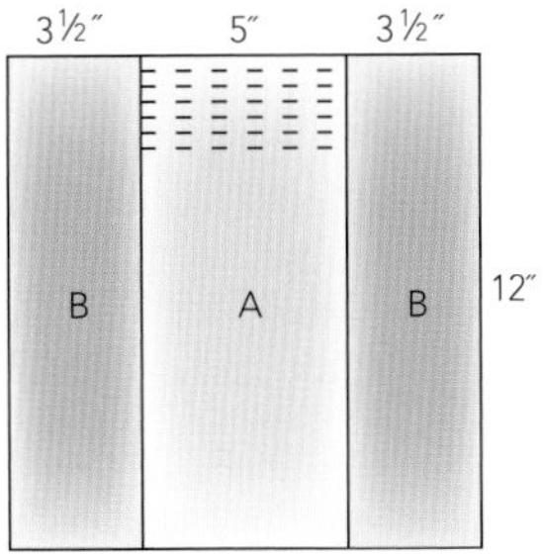

Pillow Front

PILLOW FRONT: Machine stitch across panel A, making straight parallel lines about ½″ apart. Sew a B panel to each long edge of A. Press.

ASSEMBLY: Follow the Sewing instructions on page 15.

horizontal panels

Sew this three-tone design to go with the Vertical Panels pillow shown on page 28.

Materials

PILLOW FORM	FABRIC A	FABRIC B	FABRIC C
12″ × 12″	¼ yard	¼ yard	¼ yard
16″ × 16″	¼ yard	¼ yard	½ yard
20″ × 20″	¼ yard	¼ yard	⅝ yard

Cutting Guide

PILLOW FORM	FABRIC A	FABRIC B	FABRIC C	
	PANEL A (cut 1)	BACK (cut 2)	PANEL B (cut 2)	BACK (cut 2)
12″ × 12″	4½″ × 12½″	2½″ × 12½″	6½″ × 12½″	12½″ × 8½″
16″ × 16″	5½″ × 16½″	3½″ × 16½″	8½″ × 16½″	16½″ × 10½″
20″ × 20″	6½″ × 20½″	4½″ × 20½″	10½″ × 20½″	20½″ × 12½″

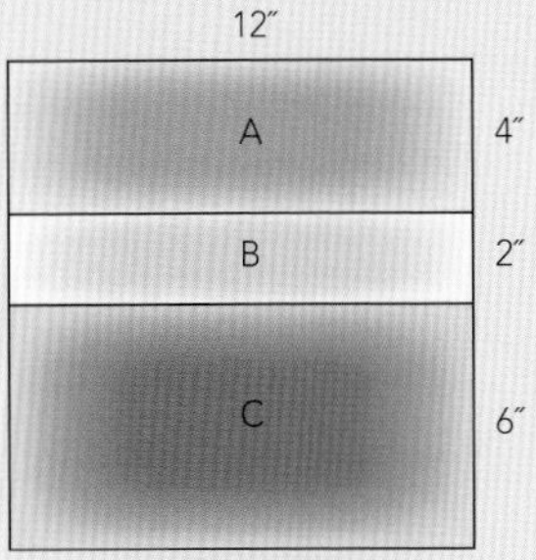

Pillow Front

PILLOW FRONT: Sew panels A, B, and C together as shown to make the pillow front. Press. Topstitch ¼″ from the seams with matching or contrasting thread.

ASSEMBLY: Follow the Sewing instructions on page 15.

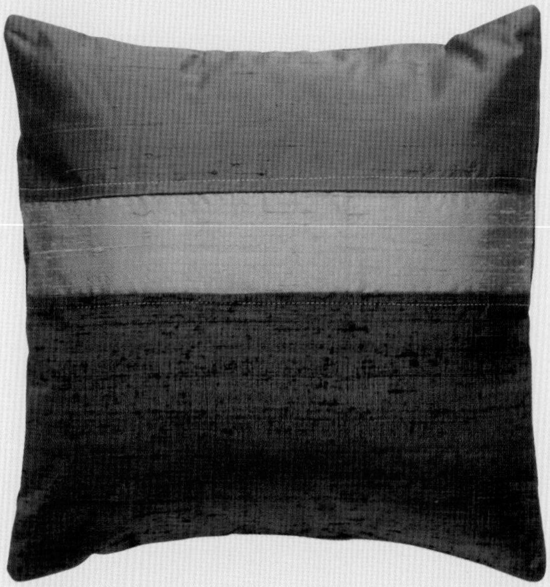

medallion

Use the diamond-shaped medallion in the center of this square pillow cover to showcase a theme print. The triangle patches at the edges are made by cutting squares diagonally in half. Each square makes two triangles. This design uses the same fabric for the pillow front and back.

Materials

PILLOW FORM	THEME PRINT	CONTRAST FABRIC	BACKGROUND FABRIC
14″ × 14″	⅓ yard	⅛ yard	⅓ yard
18″ × 18″	⅜ yard	⅛ yard	⅝ yard
24″ × 24″	½ yard	¼ yard	¾ yard

Cutting Guide

PILLOW FORM	THEME PRINT	CONTRAST FABRIC			BACKGROUND FABRIC	
	PATCH A (cut 1)	STRIP B (cut 1)	STRIP C (cut 1) STRIP D (cut 1)	STRIP E (cut 1) (cut 2 squares)	TRIANGLE F (cut 4)	BACK (cut 2)
14″ × 14″	8½″ × 8½″	1½″ × 8½″	1½″ × 9½″	1½″ × 10½″	8¼″ × 8¼″	9½″ × 14½″
18″ × 18″	10¼″ × 10¼″	2″ × 10½″	2″ × 11½″	2″ × 12½″	9⅞″ × 9⅞″	11½″ × 18½
24″ × 24″	13½″ × 13½″	2½″ × 13½″	2½″ × 15½″	2½″ × 15½″	13½″ × 13½″	14½″ × 24½″

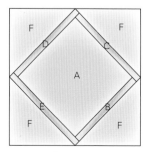

Pillow Front

PILLOW FRONT: Sew strip B to piece A. Press toward B. Sew strip C to unit AB. Press toward C. Sew strip D to unit ABC. Press. Sew strip E to unit ABCD. Press. Sew the F triangles to the outside edges of the unit. Press.

ASSEMBLY: Follow the Sewing instructions on page 15.

sashed four-patch I

Choose two fabrics for this design: a print for the main fabric and a solid or "reads-like-a-solid" for the sashing.

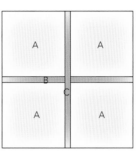

Pillow Front

PILLOW FRONT: Sew 2 A patches to strip B. Press toward B. Make 2 ABA units. Sew strip C to 1 ABA unit. Press toward C. Join the other ABA unit to strip C. Press.

ASSEMBLY: Follow the Sewing instructions on page 15.

Materials

PILLOW FORM	MAIN FABRIC	SASHING
10″ × 10″	¼ yard	⅛ yard
14″ × 14″	⅓ yard	⅛ yard
18″ × 18″	⅝ yard	⅛ yard

Cutting Guide

PILLOW FORM	MAIN FABRIC		SASHING	
	PANEL A (cut 4)	BACK (cut 2)	STRIP B (cut 2)	STRIP C (cut 1)
10″ × 10″	5″ × 5″	10½″ × 7½″	1½″ × 5″	1½″ × 10½″
14″ × 14″	7″ × 7″	14½″ × 9½″	1½″ × 7″	1½″ × 14½″
18″ × 18″	9″ × 9″	18½″ × 11½″	1½″ × 9″	1½″ × 18½″

sashed four-patch II

In this design variation, two of the patches are cut from one fabric and two are cut from another fabric. The result is a checkerboard look. Make the smallest size to use as a pincushion.

Materials

PILLOW FORM	FABRIC A	FABRIC B	SASHING
10″ × 10″	¼ yard	¼ yard	⅛ yard
14″ × 14″	⅓ yard	¼ yard	⅛ yard
18″ × 18″	⅝ yard	⅓ yard	⅛ yard
	10″ square	5″ square	2″

Cutting Guide

PILLOW FORM	FABRIC A		FABRIC B	FABRIC C	
	PATCH A (cut 2)	BACK (cut 2)	PATCH B (cut 2)	STRIP C (cut 2)	STRIP D (cut 1)
10″ × 10″	5½″ × 5½″	10½″ × 6½″	5½″ × 5½″	1½″ × 5″	1½″ × 10½″
14″ × 14″	7″ × 7″	14½″ × 10½″	7″ × 7″	1½″ × 7″	1½″ × 14½″
18″ × 18″	9″ × 9″	20½″ × 12½″	9″ × 9″	1½″ × 9″	1½″ × 18½″
	2″ × 2″	4½″ × 4½″	2″ × 2″	1″ × 2″	1″ × 4½″

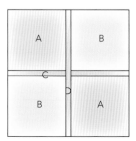

Pillow Front

PILLOW FRONT: Sew 1 A patch and 1 B patch to strip C. Press toward C. Make 2 ABC units. Sew strip D to 1 ABC unit. Press toward D. Join the other ABC unit to strip D. Press.

ASSEMBLY: Follow the Sewing instructions on page 15. Sew perle cotton or embroidery floss through the center of the pincushion and tie off the ends.

pieced border I

Patchwork squares form a jewel-toned border around a colorful batik. Using the same color sequence on each edge imparts a sense of order.

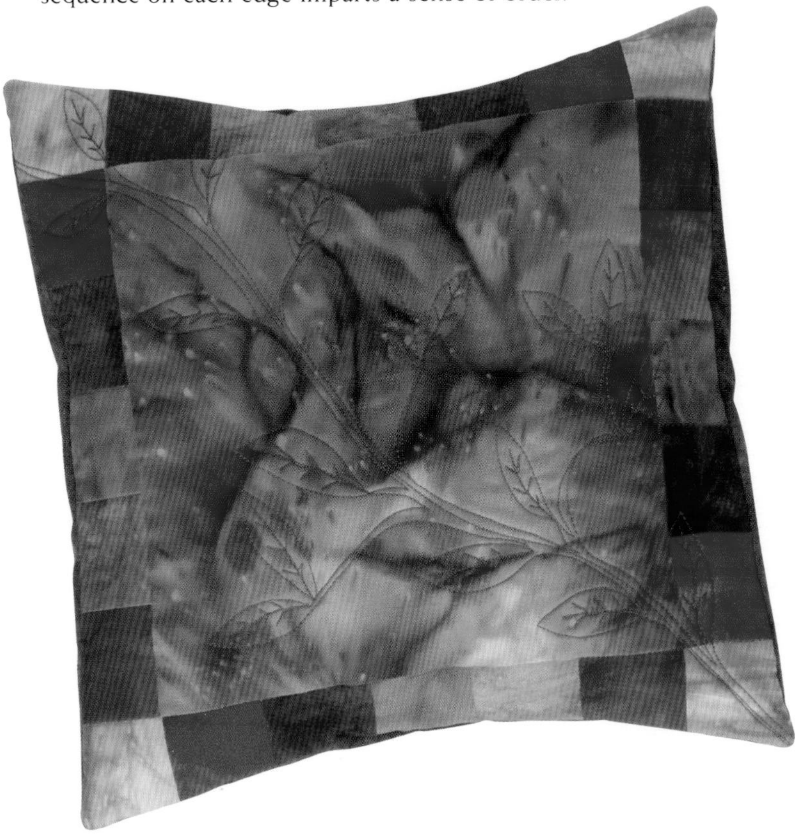

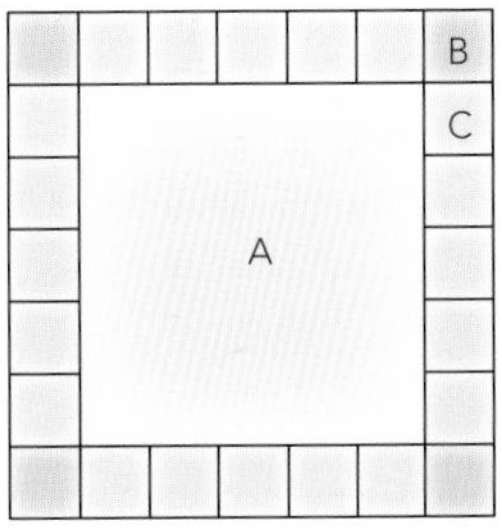

Pillow Front

PILLOW FRONT: Sew 5 different border squares together end to end. Press. Make 4 identical border strips. Sew 2 strips to the side edges of piece A. Press. Sew the B patches to the ends of the two remaining strips. Press toward B. Sew these strips to the top and bottom edges of piece A. Press.

ASSEMBLY: Follow the Sewing instructions on page 15.

Materials

PILLOW FORM	MAIN FABRIC	ACCENT FABRIC	5 ASSORTED FABRICS
10″ × 10″	¼ yard	⅛ yard	⅛ yard each
14″ × 14″	⅓ yard	⅛ yard	⅛ yard each
18″ × 18″	½ yard	⅛ yard	⅛ yard each

Cutting Guide

PILLOW FORM	MAIN FABRIC		ACCENT FABRIC	5 ASSORTED FABRICS	
	PIECE A (cut 1)	BACK (cut 2)	PATCH B (cut 4)	BORDER SQUARES (PATCH C) (cut 4 of each color, or 20 total)	
10″ × 10″	5½″ × 5½″	10½″ × 6½″	5½″ × 5½″	1½″ × 5″	1½″ × 10½″
14″ × 14″	7″ × 7″	14½″ × 10 1/12″	7″ × 7″	1½″ × 7″	1½″ × 14½″
18″ × 18″	9″ × 9″	20½″ × 12½″	9″ × 9″	1½″ × 9″	1½″ × 18½″

pieced border II

The patchwork border in this design is made of rectangles. Use a combination of light and dark colors for lively contrast. Choose colors to go with the theme fabric that appears in the middle.

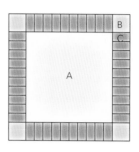

PILLOW FRONT: Sew 10 different border rectangles together side to side, alternating between light and dark color values as much as possible. Press. Make 4 identical border strips. Sew 2 strips to the side edges of piece A. Press. Sew the B patches to the ends of the two remaining strips. Press toward B. Sew these strips to the top and bottom edges of piece A. Press.

ASSEMBLY: Follow the Sewing instructions on page 15.

Materials

PILLOW FORM	FABRIC A	5 ASSORTED FABRICS
10″ × 10″	¼ yard	⅛ yard each
14″ × 14″	⅓ yard	⅛ yard each
18″ × 18″	⅝ yard	⅛ yard each

Cutting Guide

PILLOW FORM	FABRIC A			5 ASSORTED FABRICS
	PIECE A (cut 1)	PATCH B (cut 4)	BACK (cut 2)	BORDER SQUARES (PATCH C) (cut 8 of each color, or 40 total)
10″ × 10″	7½″ × 7½″	2″ × 2″	10½″ × 6½″	1½″ × 2″
14″ × 14″	10½″ × 10½″	2½″ × 2½″	14½″ × 9½″	1½″ × 2½″
18″ × 18″	12½″ × 12½″	3½″ × 3½″	18½″ × 14½″	1½″ × 3½″

triangles I

To make accurate triangle patches for this design, cut two squares from two different fabrics, following the sizes listed in the Cutting Guide. Cut each square diagonally in half in both directions to make four quarter-square triangles. Use the eight triangles to make two identical pillows, each with two colors.

Materials

PILLOW FORM (2)	FABRIC 1	FABRIC 2
10″ × 10″	⅝ yard	⅓ yard
12″ × 12″	¾ yard	½ yard
14″ × 14″	⅞ yard	½ yard
16″ × 16″	1⅛ yard	½ yard
18″ × 18″	1¼ yard	⅝ yard
20″ × 20″	1⅓ yard	¾ yard
24″ × 24″	2⅛ yard	¾ yard

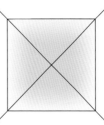

Cutting Diagram

Cutting Guide

PILLOW FORM	FABRIC 1		FABRIC 2
	TRIANGLE A (cut 4 from a square)	BACK (cut 4)	TRIANGLE B (cut 4 from a square)
10″ × 10″	11¼″ × 11¼″	10½″ × 7½″	11¼″ × 11¼″
12″ × 12″	13¼″ × 13¼″	12½″ × 8½″	13¼″ × 13¼″
14″ × 14″	15¼″ × 15¼″	14½″ × 9½″	15¼″ × 15¼″
16″ × 16″	17¼″ × 17¼″	16½″ × 10½″	17¼″ × 17¼″
18″ × 18″	19¼″ × 19¼″	18½″ × 11½″	19¼″ × 19¼″
20″ × 20″	21¼″ × 21¼″	20½″ × 12½″	21¼″ × 21¼″
24″ × 24″	25¼″ × 25¼″	24½″ × 14½″	25¼″ × 25¼″

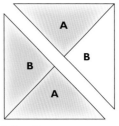

Pillow Front

PILLOW FRONTS: Arrange 2 A and 2 B triangles as shown. Sew the triangles together in pairs. Press. Join the AB pairs. Press. Sew a second pillow front to match.

ASSEMBLY: Follow the Sewing instructions on page 15.

triangles II

This design is made just like Triangles I, except four fabrics are used instead of two. For a monochromatic look, choose four graded shades, from light to dark, in the same color family. Use your leftover triangles to make additional pillows.

Materials

PILLOW FORM	FABRIC A	FABRICS B, C, D
10″ × 10″	⅓ yard	⅓ yard each
12″ × 12″	½ yard	½ yard each
14″ × 14″	½ yard	½ yard each
16″ × 16″	½ yard	⅝ yard each
18″ × 18″	1 yard	⅝ yard each
20″ × 20″	1¼ yard	¾ yard each
24″ × 24″	1½ yard	¾ yard each
30″ × 30″	1¾ yards	1 yard each

Cutting Guide

PILLOW FORM	FABRIC A		FABRIC B, C, D
	TRIANGLE A (cut 4 from a square, use 1)	BACK (cut 2)	TRIANGLES C, C, D (cut 4 from each square, use 1)
10″ × 10″	11¼″ × 11¼″	10½″ × 7½″	11¼″ × 11¼″
12″ × 12″	13¼″ × 13¼″	12½″ × 8½″	13¼″ × 13¼″
14″ × 14″	15¼″ × 15¼″	14½″ × 9½″	15¼″ × 15¼″
16″ × 16″	17¼″ × 17¼″	16½″ × 10½″	17¼″ × 17¼″
18″ × 18″	19¼″ × 19¼″	18½″ × 11½″	19¼″ × 19¼″
20″ × 20″	21¼″ × 21¼″	20½″ × 12½″	21¼″ × 21¼″
24″ × 24″	25¼″ × 25¼″	24½″ × 14½″	25¼″ × 25¼″
30″ × 30″	31¼″ × 31¼″	30½″ × 17½″	31¼″ × 31¼″

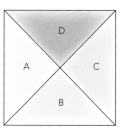

Pillow Front

PILLOW FRONT: Arrange triangles A, B, C, and D in a square, shading from light to dark as shown. Sew A to B. Press. Sew C to D. Press. Sew AB to CD. Press.

ASSEMBLY: Follow the Sewing instructions on page 15.

pillowcase style

This small accent pillow resembles a standard-size pillowcase. Make it for a 12″ × 16″ crib pillow form or a smaller 9″ × 12″ pillow form to give your bedroom a lilliputian touch.

Materials

PILLOW FORM	MAIN FABRIC	EDGE FABRIC	ACCENT FABRIC	COTTON CORD	3 BUTTONS TO COVER
9″ × 12″	⅓ yard	¼ yard	¼ yard	⅓ yard	
12″ × 16″	⅜ yard	⅓ yard	¼ yard	½ yard	

Cutting Guide

PILLOW FORM	MAIN FABRIC PIECE A (cut 1)	EDGE FABRIC PIECE B (cut 1)	BACK (cut 2)	ACCENT FABRIC STRIP FOR PIPING AND BUTTONS
9″ × 12″	9½″ × 10″	3″ × 9½″	9½″ × 8″	3″ × 18″
12″ × 16″	12½″ × 12½″	4½″ × 12½″	12½″ × 10½″	3″ × 20

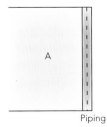

Baste the piping to edge of fabric

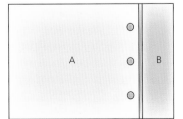

Pillow Front

PILLOW FRONT: Cover the cotton cord with the accent fabric strip (see Piping on page 23). Machine baste the piping to one short edge of piece A. Sew piece B to the same edge, enclosing the piping in the seam, to make the pillow front. Cover 3 buttons with the accent fabric. Sew them to the pillow front, about ¾″ from the piping.

ASSEMBLY: Follow the Sewing instructions on page 15.

envelope

This pillow pouch makes an unusual accent.

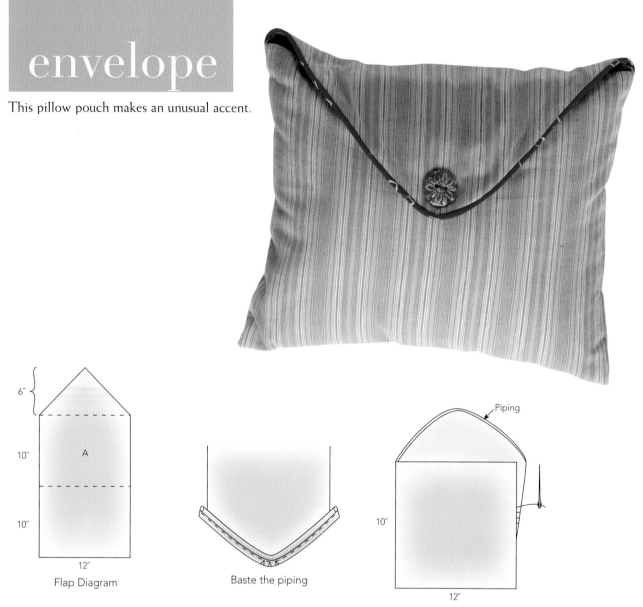

Flap Diagram

Baste the piping

Piping

Slipstitch the sides

Materials

PILLOW FORM	MAIN FABRIC	ACCENT FABRIC	COTTON CORD	1 BUTTON TO COVER, IF DESIRED
10″ × 12″	¾ yard	¼ yard	⅝ yard	

Cutting Guide

PILLOW FORM	MAIN FABRIC PIECE A (cut 2)	ACCENT FABRIC STRIP FOR PIPING	
10″ × 12″	12½″ × 26½″	2½″ × 20″	scrap to cover button

PILLOW FRONT AND BACK: Layer the 2 A pieces. Follow the diagram to mark a 6″-deep flap at one end. Cut on the marked line through both layers. Cover the cotton cord with accent fabric (see Piping on page 23). Machine baste the piping to the edge of one A flap only. Layer both A pieces, right sides together. Machine stitch all around, leaving a 3″ opening along the 12″ edge. Trim the corners, turn right side out, and slipstitch the opening.

ASSEMBLY: Fold up the bottom edge to form a 10″ × 12″ envelope pocket and slipstitch the sides. Insert the pillow form, fold down the flap, and tack. Cover a button with the accent fabric and sew it to the front flap.

double ruffle

The double ruffle is reversible and needs no hemming. Just fold the ruffle strip in half and gather both raw edges at once. To avoid a skimpy appearance, the finished width of the ruffle is about one-fourth the size of the pillow form.

Materials

PILLOW FORM	MAIN FABRIC	RUFFLE FABRIC	FLAT BRAID (OPTIONAL)
10″ × 10″	1/3 yard	1/2 yard	1 1/4 yards
12″ × 12″	1/2 yard	5/8 yard	1 1/3 yards
14″ × 14″	1/2 yard	7/8 yard	1 5/8 yards
16″ × 16″	1/2 yard	1 yard	1 7/8 yards
18″ × 18″	1 yard	1 3/8 yard	2 1/8 yards

Cutting Guide

PILLOW FORM	MAIN FABRIC		RUFFLE FABRIC
	FRONT A (cut 1)	BACK (cut 2)	DOUBLE RUFFLE (make 1 strip, piecing to obtain length)
10″ × 10″	10 1/2″ × 10 1/2″	10 1/2″ × 7 1/2″	5 1/2″ × 100″
12″ × 12″	12 1/2″ × 12 1/2″	12 1/2″ × 8 1/2″	6 1/2″ × 120″
14″ × 14″	14 1/2″ × 14 1/2″	14 1/2″ × 9 1/2″	7″ × 140″
16″ × 16″	16 1/2″ × 16 1/2″	16 1/2″ × 10 1/2″	8″ × 160″
18″ × 18″	18 1/2″ × 18 1/2″	18 1/2″ × 11 1/2″	9″ × 180″

PILLOW FRONT: Sew the ends of the ruffle strip together to make a loop. Fold the ruffle strip in half, right side out, and press. Gather the raw edges and baste them to the pillow front (see Ruffle on page 21).

ASSEMBLY: Follow the Sewing instructions on page 15. Hand sew a flat braid trim to the ruffle seam, if desired.

framed squares I

Colorful patches are arranged in two rows and surrounded by a theme print "frame." This easy patchwork design lets you play with fabric and color combinations.

Materials

PILLOW FORM	MAIN FABRIC	4 OR 5 COORDINATING SCRAPS
12″ × 22″	¾ yard	

Cutting Guide

PILLOW FORM	MAIN FABRIC			SCRAPS
	PATCH A (cut 2)	STRIP B (cut 2)	BACK (cut 2)	PATCH C (cut 14 assorted)
12″ × 22″	4½″ × 4½″	22½″ × 4½″	12½″ × 13½″	2½″ × 2½″

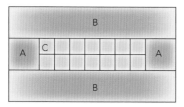

Pillow Front

PILLOW FRONT: Arrange 14 assorted C patches in 2 rows of 7 patches each. Sew the patches in each row together. Press. Sew the rows together. Press. Sew an A patch to each end. Press. Sew the B strips to the top and bottom edges. Press.

ASSEMBLY: Follow the Sewing instructions on page 15.

framed squares II

This variation places two fabric "frames" around the patchwork squares. Note how the color of the outer frame is repeated in some of the squares.

Materials

PILLOW FORM	FABRIC 1	FABRIC 2	4 COORDINATING SCRAPS
12″ × 22″	¼ yard	⅝ yard	

Cutting Guide

PILLOW FORM	FABRIC 1		FABRIC 2			SCRAPS (INCLUDING FABRIC 2)
	STRIP A (cut 2)	STRIP B (cut 2)	STRIP C (cut 2)	STRIP D (cut 2)	BACK (cut 2)	PATCH C (cut 14 assorted)
12″ × 22″	2½″ × 4½″	2½″ × 18½″	2½″ × 8½″	2½″ × 22½″	12½″ × 13½″	2½″ × 2½″

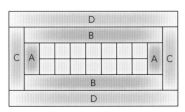

Pillow Front

PILLOW FRONT: Arrange 14 assorted C patches in 2 rows of 7 patches each. Sew the patches in each row together. Press. Sew the rows together. Press. Sew an A strip to each end. Press. Sew the B strips to the top and bottom edges. Press. Sew a C strip to each end. Press. Sew the D strips to the top and bottom edges. Press.

ASSEMBLY: Follow the Sewing instructions on page 15.

flanged four-patch

The successive frames surrounding this four-patch end in a self-flange. Choose three fabrics—light, medium, and dark—to create this graphic design.

Materials

PILLOW FORM	LIGHT FABRIC	MEDIUM FABRIC	DARK FABRIC
12″ × 12″	¼ yard	¼ yard	½ yard
18″ × 18″	¼ yard	¼ yard	¾ yard
24″ × 24″	¼ yard	¼ yard	1 yard

Cutting Guide

PILLOW FORM	LIGHT FABRIC			MEDIUM FABRIC	
	PATCH A (cut 2)	STRIP E (cut 2)	STRIP F (cut 2)	STRIP C (cut 2)	STRIP D (cut 2)
12″ × 12″	2½″ × 2½″	2½″ × 8½″	2½″ × 12½″	2½″ × 4½″	2½″ × 8½″
18″ × 18″	3½″ × 3½″	3½″ × 12½″	3½″ × 18½″	3½″ × 6½″	3½″ × 12½″
24″ × 24″	4½″ × 4½″	4½″ × 16½″	4½″ × 24½″	4½″ × 8½″	4½″ × 16½″

Cutting Guide continued

PILLOW FORM	DARK FABRIC			
	PATCH B (cut 2)	STRIP G (cut 2)	STRIP H (cut 2)	BACK (cut 2)
12″ × 12″	2½″ × 2½″	2½″ × 12½″	2½″ × 16½″	10½″ × 16½″
18″ × 18″	3½″ × 3½″	3½″ × 18½″	3½″ × 24½″	14½″ × 24½″
24″ × 24″	4½″ × 4½″	4½″ × 24½″	4½″ × 32½″	18½″ × 32½″

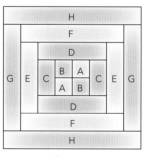

Pillow Front

PILLOW FRONT: Sew A to B. Press toward B. Make 2 AB units. Join the AB units to make a four-patch. Press. Sew the C strips to the side edges of the four-patch. Press. Sew the D strips to the top and bottom edges. Press. Add strips E, F, G, and H in pairs, pressing after each addition.

ASSEMBLY: Follow the Sewing instructions on page 15. Stitch 2 or 3 inches from the outside edge, pivoting at the corners, to make the flange (see Flange on page 20).

framed panels

A brilliant blue fabric sparks up a monochromatic palette of three greens. Try this combination with any two colors. You'll need light, medium, and dark shades of one color, plus an accent color, for four fabrics in all.

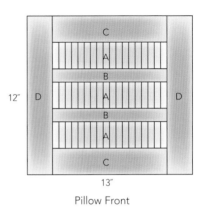

Pillow Front

PILLOW FRONT: Arrange 54 assorted A patches in 3 rows of 18 patches each. Sew the A patches together in rows. Press. Sew the A units and B strips together as shown. Press. Sew the C strips to the top and bottom edges. Press. Sew the D strips to the side edges. Press.

ASSEMBLY: Follow the Sewing instructions on page 15.

Materials

PILLOW FORM	LIGHT FABRIC	MEDIUM FABRIC	DARK FABRIC	ACCENT FABRIC
12″ × 13″	⅛ yard	⅛ yard	⅜ yard	⅛ yard

Cutting Guide

| PILLOW FORM | LIGHT PATCH A (cut 15) | MEDIUM PATCH A (cut 11) | DARK | | | | | ACCENT PATCH A (cut 17) |
			PATCH A (cut 11)	STRIP B (cut 2)	STRIP C (cut 2)	STRIP D (cut 2)	BACK (cut 2)	
12″ × 13″	1″ × 2½″	1″ × 2½″	1″ × 2½″	1½″ × 9½″	2½″ × 9½″	2½″ × 12½″	12½″ × 9″	1″ × 2½″

easy patchwork

The patchwork squares in this design were cut from scraps left over from a quilting project. To get a similar random effect with new fabrics, purchase ⅛ yard each of eight different fabrics.

Materials

PILLOW FORM	MAIN FABRIC	8 ASSORTED FABRICS
16″ × 16″	½ yard	⅛ yard each, or use scraps
20″ × 20″	1 yard	⅛ yard each, or use scraps

Cutting Guide

| PILLOW FORM | MAIN FABRIC | | | ASSORTED FABRICS |
	STRIP B (cut 2)	STRIP C (cut 2)	BACK (cut 2)	SQUARE A (cut 64)
16″ × 16″	2½″ × 12½″	2½″ × 16½″	10½″ × 16½″	2″ × 2″
20″ × 20″	2½″ × 16½″	2½″ × 20½″	12½″ × 20½″	2½″ × 2½″

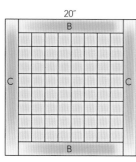

Pillow Front

PILLOW FRONT: Arrange 64 assorted A patches in 8 rows of 8 patches each. Sew the A patches together in rows. Press. Sew the rows together. Press. Sew the B strips to the top and bottom edges. Press. Sew the C strips to the side edges. Press.

ASSEMBLY: Follow the Sewing instructions on page 15.

two-for-one

Here's an efficient, economical way to make a pair of coordinated pillows.

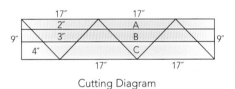

17″	17″

2″	A
3″	B
4″	C

9″ | | 9″

| 17″ | 17″ |

Cutting Diagram

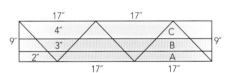

17″	17″

4″	C
3″	B
2″	A

9″ | | 9″

| 17″ | 17″ |

Cutting Diagram

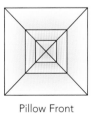

Pillow Front   Pillow Front

PILLOW FRONTS (2): Sew strips A, B, and C together as shown. Press. Make 2 ABC strip sets. Rotate 1 strip set as shown, so that strip C is at the top. Use a quilter's ruler to mark a series of 45° angles on each strip set. Cut on the marked lines to make 4 triangles with strip A on the outside and 4 triangles with strip C on the outside. Arrange 4 matching triangles into a square. Sew the triangles together in pairs. Press. Join the pairs. Make 2 pillow fronts.

ASSEMBLY: Follow the Sewing instructions on page 15.

Materials

PILLOW FORM	FABRIC A	FABRIC B	FABRIC C
16″ × 16″ (2)	¼ yard	¼ yard	¾ yard

Cutting Guide

PILLOW FORM	FABRIC A STRIP A (cut 2)	FABRIC B STRIP B (cut 2)	FABRIC C STRIP C (cut 2)	BACK (cut 4)
16″ × 16″	2½″ × 42″	3½″ × 42″	4½″ × 42″	10½″ × 16½″

pieced rectangle

Use the center panel of this rectangular pillow cover to showcase a theme print or novelty fabric. Two other fabrics in coordinating colors complete the design.

Materials

PILLOW FORM	FABRIC A	FABRIC B	FABRIC C
12″ × 22″	¼ yard	¼ yard	⅜ yard

Cutting Guide

PILLOW FORM	FABRIC A	FABRIC B	FABRIC C	
	STRIP A (cut 1)	STRIP B (cut 2)	STRIP C (cut 2)	BACK (cut 2)
12″ × 22″	6½″ × 12½″	4½″ × 12½″	4½″ × 12½″	13½″ × 12½″

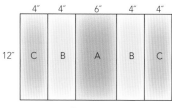

Pillow Front

PILLOW FRONT: Sew a B strip to each long edge of strip A. Press. Sew a C strip to each B strip. Press.

ASSEMBLY: Follow the Sewing instructions on page 15.

log cabin I

A Log Cabin block is made by sewing strips of fabric around a center square. The strips fall into light and dark areas that divide the block diagonally in half. Cut the center square for each block from one fabric, such as the bright red used in the rectangular pillow. To further unify the design, cut matching sets of strips, as in the square pillow. The blocks can be rotated to achieve different patterns for the pillow front.

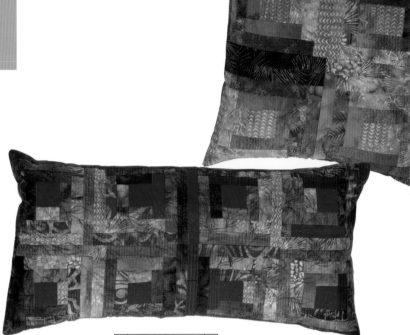

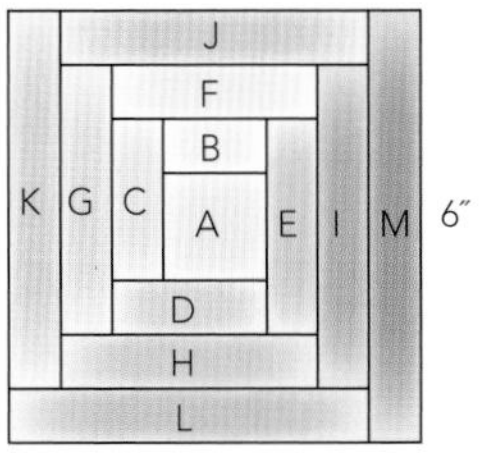

Materials

PILLOW FORM	CENTER PATCH (LIGHT OR DARK)	ASSORTED LIGHTS	ASSORTED DARKS (INLCUDES BACK)
12″ × 12″	2″ × 2″ piece	¼ yard total	½ yard total
18″ × 18″	2″ × 2″ piece	½ yard total	⅝ yard total
12″ × 22″	2″ × 2″ piece	½ yard total	⅝ yard total

Block Piecing Diagram   4 blocks

8 blocks

9 blocks

Pillow Diagrams

Cutting Guide

PILLOW FORM (# of blocks)	CENTER PATCH	ASSORTED LIGHTS STRIPS	ASSORTED DARKS STRIPS	BACK (cut 2)
	A 2″ × 2″	B 1¼″ × 2″	D 1¼″ × 2¾″	
		C 1¼″ × 2¾″	E 1¼″ × 3½″	
		F 1¼″ × 3½″	H 1¼″ × 4¼″	
		G 1¼″ × 4¼″	I 1¼″ × 5″	
		J 1¼″ × 5″	L 1¼″ × 5¾″	
		K 1¼″ × 5¾″	M 1¼″ × 6½″	
12″ × 12″ (4 blocks)	Cut 4 matching	Cut 4 of each strip, assorted or matching		12½″ × 8½″
18″ × 18″ (9 blocks)	Cut 9 matching	Cut 9 of each strip, assorted or matching		18½″ × 11½″
12″ × 22″ (8 blocks)	Cut 8 matching	Cut 8 of each strip, assorted or matching		12½″ × 14½″

SINGLE BLOCK: Sew strip B to square A. Press. Sew strip C to AB. Press. Sew strip D to ABC. Press. Add strips E through M in the same way, moving counterclockwise around the center unit, to make one 6″ × 6″ block.

PILLOW FRONT: Make the number of blocks required for the pillow size. Arrange the blocks as shown in the diagram. Sew the blocks together in rows. Press. Join the rows. Press.

ASSEMBLY: Follow the Sewing instructions on page 15.

log cabin II

Here's another version of the Log Cabin block. Three different colors are used. The pieced strips form solid bands of color around each center square.

Materials

PILLOW FORM	LIGHT FABRIC	MEDIUM FABRIC	DARK FABRIC
12″ × 12″	⅛ yard	⅛ yard	⅓ yard
18″ × 18″	¼ yard	⅓ yard	½ yard
12″ × 22″	¼ yard	⅓ yard	½ yard

Cutting Guide

PILLOW FORM (# of blocks)	LIGHT CENTER PATCH	LIGHT STRIPS	MEDIUM STRIPS	DARK CENTER PATCH	DARK STRIPS	BACK
	A 2″ × 2″	B 1¼″ × 2″	B 1¼″ × 2″	A 2″ × 2″	F 1¼″ × 3½″	
		C 1¼″ × 2¾″	C 1¼″ × 2¾″		G 1¼″ × 4¼″	
		D 1¼″ × 2¾″	D 1¼″ × 2¾″		H 1¼″ × 4¼″	
		E 1¼″ × 3½″	E 1¼″ × 3½″		I 1¼″ × 5″	
		J 1¼″ × 5″	J 1¼″ × 5″			
		K 1¼″ × 5¾″	K 1¼″ × 5¾″			
		L 1¼″ × 5¾″	L 1¼″ × 5¾″			
		M 1¼″ × 6½″	M 1¼″ × 6½″			
12″ × 12″ (4 blocks)	Cut 2	Cut 2 of each strip	Cut 2 of each strip	Cut 2	Cut 4 of each strip	12½″ × 8½″
18″ × 18″ (9 blocks)	Cut 5	Cut 5 of each strip	Cut 5 of each strip	Cut 4	Cut 9 of each strip	18½″ × 11½″
12″ × 22″ (8 blocks)	Cut 4	Cut 4 of each strip	Cut 4 of each strip	Cut 4	Cut 8 of each strip	12½″ × 14½″

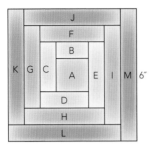

Block 1 Piecing Diagram

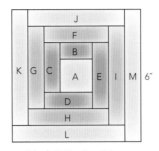

Block 2 Piecing Diagram

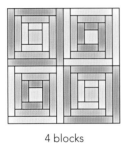

4 blocks

8 blocks

9 blocks

Pillow Diagrams

BLOCK 1: Sew a light strip B to a dark square A. Press. Sew a light strip C to AB. Press. Sew a light strip D to ABC. Press. Sew a light strip E to ABCD. Press. Add dark strips F, G, H, and I and medium strips J, K, L, and M, pressing after each addition.

BLOCK 2: Sew a medium strip B to a light square A. Press. Sew a medium strip C to AB. Press. Sew a medium strip D to ABC. Press. Sew a medium strip E to ABCD. Press. Add dark strips F, G, H, and I and light strips J, K, L, and M, pressing after each addition.

PILLOW FRONT: Make the required number of each block for your pillow size. Arrange the blocks as shown in the diagram. Sew the blocks together in rows. Press. Join the rows. Press.

ASSEMBLY: Follow the Sewing instructions on page 15.

wool circles

This pillow is made entirely of felted wool (see How to Felt Wool on page 12). The circles are cut in three sizes and various colors, layered atop one another, and sewn by hand with blanket stitch. The result is a warm and informal folk-art look.

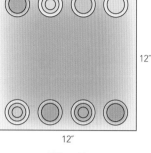

Blanket Stitch

Pillow Front

PILLOW FRONT: Layer the B and/or C circles on top of the A circles to form various color combinations. Arrange the layered circles, evenly spaced, across the top and bottom edges of the pillow front, 1½″ to 2″ from the edges. Pin. Thread a size 9 hand-embroidery needle with perle cotton. Work blanket stitch around the edge of each circle through all layers.

ASSEMBLY: Follow the Sewing instructions on page 15.

Materials

PILLOW FORM	MAIN COLOR	ASSORTED ACCENT COLORS	SIZE 8 PERLE COTTON
12″ × 12″	⅜ yard	six 3″ × 9″ pieces	1 skein
16″ × 16″	½ yard	nine 3″ × 9″ pieces	1 skein
20″ × 20″	1 yard	twelve 3″ × 9″ pieces	1 skein

Cutting Guide

PILLOW FORM	MAIN COLOR		ASSORTED ACCENT COLORS		
	FRONT (cut 1)	BACK (cut 2)	A	B	C
12″ × 12″	12½″ × 12½″	12½″ × 8½″	Cut 8	Cut 5	Cut 6
16″ × 16″	16½″ × 16½″	16½″ × 10½″	Cut 10	Cut 6	Cut 7
20″ × 20″	20½″ × 20½″	20½″ × 12½″	Cut 12	Cut 7	Cut 9

B

A

C

Follow the Cutting Guide and use patterns A, B, and C to cut the required number of circles from felted wool.

buttons

Make this rectangular accent pillow to showcase new or vintage buttons. The panels are cut from wool felt (see How to Felt Wool on page 12). Choose a color for panel A that offers good contrast against the buttons.

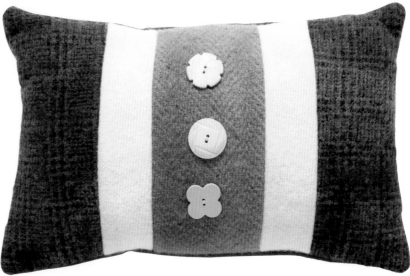

Materials

PILLOW FORM	WOOL FELT 1	WOOL FELT 2	WOOL FELT 3	BUTTONS
7½″ × 12″	⅛ yard	⅛ yard	¼ yard	3

Cutting Guide

PILLOW FORM	WOOL FELT 1 PANEL A (cut 1)	WOOL FELT 2 PANEL B (cut 2)	WOOL FELT 3 PANEL C (cut 2)	WOOL FELT 3 BACK (cut 2)	BUTTONS
7½″ × 12″	3½″ × 8″	2″ × 8″	3½″ × 8″	7½″ × 8½″	3

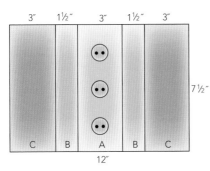

Pillow Front

PILLOW FRONT: Sew a B panel to each side of panel A. Press. Sew a C panel to each end of the BAB unit. Press. Center the buttons on panel A and hand sew in place.

ASSEMBLY: Follow the Sewing instructions on page 15.

whipstitched squares

The felted wool squares in this pillow are whipstitched together. The stitching shows on the face of the pillow, for informal texture. Some quilt shops sell prepackaged felt wool squares—a more economical way than buying fabric by the yard to get a variety of colors. You can also make your own felted wool (see How to Felt Wool on page 12).

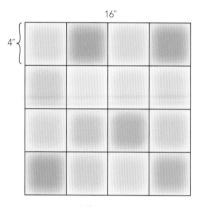

Pillow Front

Whip stitch

PILLOW FRONT: Arrange 16 patches in 4 rows of 4 squares each. Thread a size 9 hand-embroidery needle with cotton floss or wool yarn. Lift 2 adjacent squares from the top row, layer them wrong sides together, and whipstitch one edge. Whipstitch the remaining patches in the top row. Repeat for the remaining rows. Then whipstitch the rows together.

ASSEMBLY: Follow the Sewing instructions on page 15.

Materials

PILLOW FORM	MAIN COLOR	7 ACCENT COLORS	ASSORTED COTTON FLOSS OR WOOL YARN
16˝ × 16˝	⅓ yard	⅛ yard each	

Cutting Guide

PILLOW FORM	MAIN COLOR		7 ACCENT COLORS
	BACK (cut 2)	PATCHES (cut 2)	PATCHES (cut 2)
16˝ × 16˝	16½˝ × 10½˝	4½˝ × 4½˝	4½˝ × 4½˝

whipstitched pincushion

Use scraps of wool felt to make this practical pincushion.

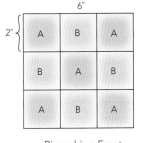

Pincushion Front

Whip stitch

PINCUSHION FRONT: Arrange the A and B patches in a nine-patch as shown. Thread a size 9 hand-embroidery needle with cotton floss or wool yarn. Lift an A and a B square from the top row, layer them wrong sides together, and whipstitch one edge. Whipstitch the remaining A patch to B to complete the row. Repeat for the remaining rows. Then whipstitch the rows together.

ASSEMBLY: Layer the front and back wrong sides together. Whipstitch around 3 sides. Stuff firmly with fiberfill, then whipstitch closed.

Materials and Cutting Guide

SIZE	DARK WOOL FELT		LIGHT WOOL FELT	FIBERFILL
	PATCH A (cut 5)	BACK (cut 1)	PATCH B (cut 4)	
4½″ × 4½″	2″ × 2″	5″ × 5″	2″ × 2″	

Materials and Cutting Guide

SIZE	ASSORTED SILK SCRAPS		FIBERFILL, LAVENDER, OR OTHER STUFFING MATERIAL
	PATCHES (cut 16)	BACK (cut 1)	
4″ × 4″	1½″ × 1½″	4½″ × 4½″	

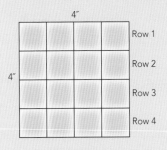

Pillow Front

silk pincushion

Sew this petite pillow from scraps of silk fabric. Stuff it with fiberfill to make a pincushion. Add a dry herb, such as lavender, for a sweet-smelling sachet.

PILLOW FRONT: Arrange 16 assorted patches in 4 rows of 4 patches each. Sew the patches together in rows. Press the seams in rows 1 and 3 in one direction. Press the seams in rows 2 and 4 in the opposite direction. Sew the rows together. Press.

ASSEMBLY: Layer the front and back right sides together. Stitch all around, leaving a 2″ opening on one edge. Turn right side out. Stuff firmly. Slipstitch the opening.

pillowcase

Make the pillow you use every night extra special with theme prints and accent fabrics. Sewing your own pillowcases is an inexpensive way to add a custom touch to your family's bedding.

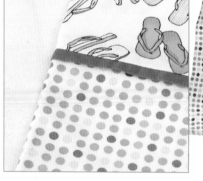

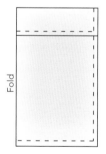

Materials

SIZE	THEME FABRIC	EDGE FABRIC	ACCENT FABRIC
20″ × 26″ (standard)	¾ yard	⅓ yard	⅛ yard
20″ × 30″ (queen)	1 yard	⅓ yard	⅛ yard
20″ × 36″ (king)	1¼ yard	⅓ yard	⅛ yard

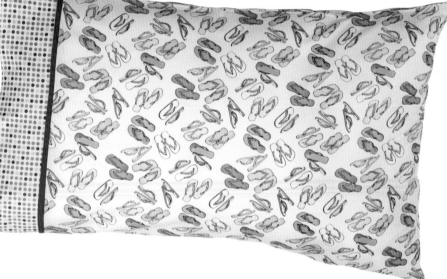

Accent Strip

Joining the pieces

Sewing the pieces

Cutting Guide

SIZE	THEME FABRIC A (cut 1)	EDGE FABRIC B (cut 1)	ACCENT FABRIC C (cut 1)
20″ × 26″ (standard)	26″ × 41″	9″ × 41″	1½″ × 41″
20″ × 30″ (queen)	30″ × 41″	9″ × 41″	1½″ × 41″
20″ × 36″ (king)	36″ × 41″	9″ × 41″	1½″ × 41″

JOINING THE PIECES: Fold strip B in half lengthwise, right side out, and press. Repeat for strip C. Place C on the right side of rectangle A, raw edges matching. Layer B on top, raw edges matching. Stitch ½″ from the edge through all layers. Trim the seam allowance to ¼″ and zigzag or overcast the raw edge.

SEWING THE SEAMS: Fold the work in half, wrong side out, with edges matching. Stitch the side and bottom edges, using a ½″ seam allowance and pivoting at the corner. Trim and overcast the seam allowance. Turn right side out and press.

gallery

basic square

Basic Square with corded edge pages 22 and 28

vertical panels

stitched panel

| Oh Sew Easy Pillows

medallion

horizontal panels

log cabin I

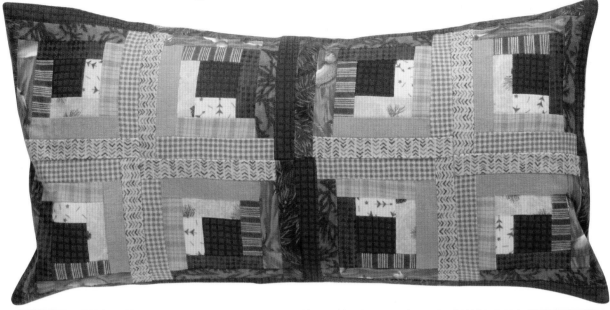

sashed four-patch I

sashed four-patch II

two-for-one

Double Ruffle
page 21

pillowcase

Pillowcase
page 54